Psychological Influence

Power of Persuasion

Dan Miller

Table of Contents

Important Insight

Almost everyone can admit that at one time or the other, they have been tricked or pushed into something because of naivety or the power of influence. For whichever motive, we have been an easy target for the pitches of fundraisers, peddlers and operators of one type or the other. While some of these people have good motives, a few of them may have dishonorable intensions.

Whenever you find yourself in possession of unwanted subscriptions of newspapers, magazines or even newsletters, someone must have persuaded you into filling in your details even though you did not have an interest from the start.

This opens up the debate on the issue of compliance and the factors that can cause you to say yes to another person because of the techniques and language that they use to convince you. If you have been keen enough, there is a certain way in which a request is stated if it is to be successful. A slight alteration may see the request rejected.

Social psychologists have researched intensely on the psychology of compliance. Some of these studies have included laboratory experiments while others have involved field experiments where real people have been interviewed to shed light on the power of persuasion.

There are principles that influence the tendency to say yes to a request. Knowing these principles and how they work is instrumental if you are to excel in the discipline of persuasion.

Contrary to what many people believe, the psychology of influence is a preserve of the elite and a certain section of the society. The truth is that we all need to learn on how to harness the power of persuasion.

This is because our daily lives revolve around bargains of one sort or the other. In the same way, we fall victim to the persuasions of other people at least to some degree in our interaction with friends, neighbors and family. To be competent in the mastery of compliance, you need more than just an amateurish and vague understanding of how persuasion works.

As you read this book, you will gain a unique insight into the strategies and techniques that are effective in the psychology of influence.

1: Understanding the Weapons of Influence

In the words of Alfred North Whitehead, *civilization advances by extending the number of operations we can perform without thinking about them*. There is a principle of human behavior which says that when you ask someone to do you a favor, your chances of success will be higher if you accompany the request with a reason.

In a study done by Ellen Langer, a social psychologist together with her co-workers, a certain form of human automaticity was demonstrated. Generally, people want to have a reason for everything that they do. In her experiment, Langer asked a small group of people who were waiting in line to use a copying machine, for a small favor.

She explained to them that she wanted to be excused because she was in a rush and she needed 5 pages copied. Because of her tagged request, 94 percent of those she asked accepted her request to skip ahead of the line.

Still in the same study, she made the same request but this time round she did not give a reason why she should be given the chance to use the machine ahead of the rest. Only 60 percent accepted to let her have the right of way. What this means is that reason triggers and justifies compliance.

The psychology of influence may not necessarily work within the confines of conventional behavior. For instance, assume a sales person who has been struggling to make a sale one day wakes up and doubles the price of the merchandise and puts a poster which says hurry while supplies last!

This is most likely to trigger a different response to the positive where customers may come flocking in just to get a piece of the same merchandise that they had not bought while it was selling at a lower price.

The automatic behavior of humans is learned more than inborn. It is more flexible compared to the automatic response witnessed in lower animals which tends to be in lock-step patterns. The simple usage of the word "because" can dramatically change the course of events and bring compliance where there should have been none.

Researchers have uncovered impressive similarities in courtship patterns exhibited across many different cultures. For example, in personal ads displayed on the internet or in newspapers, women tend to describe their physical attractiveness while men on the other hand speak of their material wealth.

The Shortcut Odds

In life, there is a rule that says "you get what you pay for". With time, this rule was also translated to mean "expensive is always good". This is however not true in all circumstances. In some situations, you can deliberately exploit the power of psychology to make people pay a heavy price on your item over and above its worth.

Instead of going through each feature of the products we buy, we tend to take shortcuts and use the price as the first and final determinant of value. We all exist in an extraordinarily complicated society that is rapidly moving.

In order to deal with its pace, we tend to leverage on shortcuts. Most times we justify our actions on the fact that there exists many variables and it is almost impossible to master and keep track of each feature of a product and how it connects to its value.

The shortcut, automated and stereotype behavior is common in human action because at times it is the most efficient way of behaving and in other instances it is simply necessary. Because of our lack of time, capacity or energy to analyze all aspects in a person, situation or event, we tend to use our rules of thumb to try and classify things based on a few features and then condition our response without thinking much.

Psychologists have discovered certain mental shortcuts that we use in making judgments on a daily basis. Among these shortcuts include:

Termed Judgmental Heuristics

This refers to shortcuts which work almost in the same manner as the way "expensive is always good" rule. It allows for a simplified thinking which although works in certain situations, but occasionally opens us up to costly mistakes.

For instance, consider those heuristics which tell you to believe what you are told as long as it is from a position of authority. This exposes you to unsettling tendencies where you accept without thinking, directions and statements that come from authoritative individuals. Rather than thinking about the arguments put forward by the expert, there is likelihood to ignore them and instead be convinced by the mere status of the expert.

Since in this situation we tend to respond mechanically to one piece of information, it is referred to as automatic responding. Controlled responding on the other hand involves a thorough analysis of all available information and perspectives before making a decision.

Laboratory research has clearly brought out the fact that people engage in controlled responding when they have the ability and desire to analyze the different aspects involved. When this desire is lacking, the automatic responding is often the best alternative.

Petty, Cacioppo and Goldman 1981 Study

To investigate automatic responding and controlled responding, Petty, Cacioppo and Goldman carried out a study in the University of Missouri. In this study, the students were required to listen to a recorded speech which was explaining in support of the requirement for all seniors to pass comprehensive examinations if they were to graduate. Some of the listeners were affected in an individual capacity because the directive was to take effect the following year. Because of this, they sat down and analyzed the arguments put forward carefully.

The other group that was unaffected, attached less personal importance, hence they did not have a strong need to digest the argument and measure its validity. From this study, it was concluded that the absence of a personal stake in a topic can easily arouse disinterest. This makes it easy to go with the rule; if an expert says so, then it must be true.

The Profiteers

Due to our automatic responding patterns, people have taken advantage of them for their own benefit. These are the profiteers. They mimic the trigger features of our automatic responding and use our naivety to gain advantage and a foothold where they should have not.

Since birth, we have grown to learn and accept some psychological principles that direct our human action, though in varying degrees. Because of this early exposure, we have been subjected to these stereotypes and they have persuasively moved us without really thinking about their power. In the eyes of other people, each of these principles is a ready weapon of automatic influence.

Profiteers are people who know where the weapons of automatic influence are and as such they expertly and regularly employ them to get what they want. They go from one social encounter to another, requesting people to comply with their wishes and believe it or not, their frequency of success is amazing.

They know how to structure their requests and they arm themselves with one or more weapons of influence which exist in the social environment. To achieve this, they correctly choose one word that engages a key psychology principle that sets the rest of the automatic behavior tapes rolling for their own benefit.

As it is in the Japanese martial arts jujitsu, where you employ minimal personal strength and exploit the power of leverage, gravity, inertia and momentum to defeat a physically stronger rival. Profiteers operate in the same manner. They commission the power of the weapons of influence against their targets while using little personal force. This gives enormous additional benefit of manipulating without the appearance of manipulation. The victims on their part do not see their compliance as an action of the profiteer but a result of natural forces.

The Contrast Principle of Human Perception

This principle affects the manner in which we see the difference between two things based on their order of presentation. A simple explanation of this principle is that if the second item is slightly different from the first, chances are that you will see it more different than it actually is.

For instance, if you lift an object which is light in weight first and thereafter lift a heavy object, you will tend to overestimate the weight of the second object than it would have been the case had you started by lifting it first.

This principle is well established in the area of psychological influence and applies to every perception. If you happen to talk to a very attractive individual and thereafter be joined by one who is not as attractive, you will tend to overstate their unattractiveness more than it actually is.

The weapon of influence provided by this principle has been exploited by a number of individuals. The most striking thing is that this principle is virtually undetectable. It gives people who cash in on this amazing technique any trace of suspicion that they have structured the situation to their favor.

Marketers often capitalize on this principle by showing customers the most expensive items first then the cheaper one later. The common sense here is that if you buy the expensive item, chances are that you will buy the next item which is slightly cheaper because in your perspective, it will look cheaper than it actually is.

In the real estate field, the principle of contrast is also widely used where a salesman starts by showing you a couple of undesirable houses which are commonly known as setup properties. These houses are ideally not meant for sale rather they were there just to be shown to the customers so as to benefit the company from the comparison with its inventory of genuine properties.

Therefore much of the compliance process can be well understood in terms of the individual tendencies to adopt shortcut and automatic responding. Many people have developed trigger features for compliance. They have a set of certain pieces of information which inform them when the compliance to a certain request is likely to be beneficial and correct. In the psychology of influence, each of these triggers can be used as a weapon of influence to stimulate your audience to agree and execute your request.

2: An In-Depth Look on the Rule of Reciprocation

The rule of reciprocation is one of the most potent weapons of influence. This rule states that we should repay kindly in what another person has given us. If someone offers you a favor, you should return the favor. For instance, if a couple invites you to a party, be sure to invite them also.

The reciprocity rule makes us obligated to the future repayment of gifts, invitations, favors among other things. This is probably why instead of saying thank you, people tend to use the phrase - much obliged - in acknowledging the receipt of things.

The aspect of reciprocation is so widespread in the human culture that sociologists including Alvin Gouldner, among others, reported through studies that all human societies subscribe to this rule. Within the society, the pervasiveness of reciprocation permeates every sort of exchange. Richard Leakey, an archeologist, ascribes the essence of what it means to be human to the system of reciprocity.

In his argument, Leakey puts it that we are humans because our ancestors knew the meaning of sharing skills and foods through an honored network of obligation.

Cultural anthropologists on the other hand view the web of indebtedness as a human adaptive mechanism that allows for the division of labor, the creation of binding interdependencies among individuals and the exchange of different forms of goods and services.

There are certain societies that have formalized the reciprocity rule into a ritual. This is true for the Vartan Bhanji, a customized form of gift exchange that is common in parts of India and Pakistan. Guests to an occasion of marriage are given gifts when they are about to leave as a form of appreciation or some kind of repayment for the good they have done.

How the Reciprocity Rule Works

The human society derives a significant competitive advantage from the rule of reciprocity. As a matter of fact, each one of us has been trained by society to comply with this rule failure to which some social sanctions were applied.

Because of the general distaste associated with people who take and make no effort to reciprocate, we often go to extra lengths in order to avoid being classified as ingrates, moochers or freeloaders. It is on this premise that certain individuals through the power of psychological influence posed by reciprocity often take us in and gain from our indebtedness.

Dennis Regan Experiment

In order to understand this rule and how it can be exploited as a weapon of influence, it is important to examine the experiment conducted by Dennis Regan, a psychologist. In the study, one participant who was also Dr. Regan's assistant, rated together with others the quality of some paintings which were part of an exhibition.

In random instances, the assistant-participant did some small unsolicited favors to the main subjects. In one of the short rest periods, the assistant came into the room with some bottles of soft drinks to distribute to the subjects and one for him. In other situations, the assistant went for a break and came back empty handed. Later in the experiment, the assistant started selling raffle tickets.

According to the findings, the subjects who had benefitted from his earlier favors purchased the tickets without any hesitation. Although this seems to be a simple demonstration, it clearly shows us the mechanics behind the rule of reciprocity.

Reciprocation is Powerful

The reason why reciprocation is such an effective weapon of influence in gaining compliance is because of its power. It possesses strength which often produces a positive response to a request which would have been declined were it not for the feeling of indebtedness occasioned by reciprocation.

In the Regan study above, it was also revealed that the reciprocity rule has a force that overpowers the influence of other factors which determine compliance with a request. For instance, Regan investigated how liking for a person can affect your tendency to comply with his request. The likelihood of people buying tickets because they liked the assistant-participant was very high.

In the sales and marketing field, the reciprocity rule has such a huge impact. When marketing to people who ordinarily dislike you, you can greatly enhance your chances of making a sale or causing your audience to do what you want by providing them with a small favor before making such a request.

Reciprocity Rule Case Study – The Hare Krishna Society Fundraising

There is a spectacular historical example of reciprocity where the Hare Krishna Society experienced a remarkable growth in wealth, property and followers. This was due to generous contributions and the efforts by both the society's members and passersby in public places. In its earlier operations, the Society solicited for contributions through its groups of Krishna devotees who canvassed city streets, bobbing and chanting in unison while begging for finances.

This method attracted a lot of attention but unfortunately it did not work well for fundraising. Most donors considered them weird and therefore reluctant to give them money.

The Society quickly noted the existence of a public relation problem where the people being asked for contribution did not quite approve the way the members dressed, looked or acted. Because of the inherent reluctance to change seen in religious organizations, the Krishna leadership found itself in a real dilemma.

On one hand, there were modes of dress, belief systems and hairstyles that had a huge religious significance. On the other, was a financial threatening situation which had the potential to grind the organization's activities to a halt.

The resolution made by the Krishna leadership was excellent. They switched their fundraising tactic such that their target donors did not necessarily need to have positive feelings towards the fundraisers. They employed a donor request procedure which engaged the rule of reciprocation.

This new strategy involved soliciting contributions in high traffic corridors such as airports and affluent streets. Before the donation request was presented, the target donor was given a small gift such as a book or a cost effective version of a flower.

The unsuspecting passersby found themselves with flowers placed into their hands as well as pinned to their jackets with no option of giving them back because the Krishna fundraisers insisted it was just a gift. After the target accepted the gift, the Krishna member would then ask for a small favor in form of a donation and in most cases the person's would give without hesitation.

This strategy commonly known as the bene-factor-before-beggar approach was wildly successful in raising funds for the Hare Krishna Society. They were able to make significant economic gains and the funding was used for building temples, houses, businesses and property in about 321 centers all over the United States and abroad.

Politics and Reciprocation

Politics is an interesting arena where the power of reciprocity is imbued in every tactic used by the politicians. At the top, the elected officials engage in an exchange of favors and logrolling which makes politics an appropriate space for strange bedfellows.

One elected representative can make an out-of-character vote on a bill sponsored by a colleague as a favor which is to be returned later on when the member bills his own bill on the floor for voting.

As a matter of fact, political analysts are amazed at how some of the programs brought before the Congress sail through even by members who are seen as direct and strong opponents to the proposals. A close examination of this political trend found that some of the savvy politicians are able to amass huge scores of favors which they then use to support their own bills.

In organizational politics, senior officials in corporations may give favors to legislative and judicial officials in exchange for the lifting of legal restrictions against the corporations. It is almost natural that when you give a favor, you are putting the recipient in a state of indebtedness.

In political setups, rarely do political figures admit that the campaign contributions. The free trips and niceties have the power to sway the opinions of the electorate or other government officials. The recipients are often disguised as being mature, smart and sophisticated enough to be affected by the small favors and gifts.

Reciprocity as a Marketing Technique

Marketing using free samples has a long and effective history. In the merchandising field, manufacturers and some large wholesalers give a small amount of the relevant product to the target consumers so as to expose the qualities of the product to the target audience.

These free samples also serve as a gift and this is the point where they engage the reciprocity rule. For instance, most Jujitsu promoters provide free samples to release a natural force which is inherent in the samples. However on the outside, these samples are seen as an innocent gesture with an intention to inform.

Another favorite place where free samples are mostly used is the supermarket. Customers are given small amounts of a product to try so as to receive a feedback. Many of these customers find it difficult to just accept the samples from the attendants without buying some of the products even if they may not have liked it much.

Therefore, the reciprocity rule governs lots of situations which are purely interpersonal in nature and where no commercial exchange or money is at issue.

One of the most captivating accounts of reciprocation as a weapon of influence comes from a scene in World War I where a German soldier responsible for capturing enemy soldiers for interrogation failed to capture a lone soldier simply because of a gift of bread. The German soldier who had negotiated skillfully to the enemy territory came across a lone enemy soldier in his trench.

The unsuspecting enemy soldier was eating at the time and therefore became an easy target for disarmament. The frightened captive in possession of only a piece of bread performed an act that saved his life. He gave the German soldier a piece of the bread. This moved the soldier and as a result he could not complete his mission. He did not capture the soldier, re-crossed back to his territory empty-handed ready to face the wrath of his seniors.

Reciprocity Enforces Uninvited Debts

You can trigger a feeling of indebtedness by simply doing an uninvited favor. This is a phenomenon that was studied by Paese and Gilin in 2000. Remember the reciprocity rule states that we should give to others through the same kindness we were provided.

It does not matter whether you asked for the favor in order to honor the obligation to repay. The American Disabled Veterans organization observed that its simple mailing program appealing for donations receives about 18 percent response rate. However, when the same mailing approach is integrated with an unsolicited gift boosts the success rate to over 35 percent.

The social purpose of the reciprocity rule is to promote the development of reciprocal relationships among individuals so that one party can confidently initiate such a relationship without fearing for any loss. In describing the social pressures around gift-giving processes, the French anthropologist, Marcel Mauss concluded that the human culture consists of obligations to give, obligations to receive and obligations to repay.

The obligation to receive automatically reduces our ability to choose the people we wish to be indebted to and as such put the power in the hands of others. The extent to which an uninvited favor produces indebtedness once received is illustrated aptly in the soliciting technique exhibited by the Hare Krishna Society. Even though some of the people who received the unsolicited gifts threw them away later on, this did not limit the effectiveness of the gift in raising the donation at the first opportunity.

In many of the gifts received with an original intention of supporting a charitable course or returning a favor, the solicitor normally accompanies the gift with a note saying that the goods are just but a gift and any money sent should not be regarded as a payment but rather as an encouragement or a return offering.

The Reciprocity Rule Triggers Unequal Exchanges

The unequal exchange feature in the reciprocity rule makes it easy to be exploited for profit. Initially, the rule was designed so as to promote equal exchanges between parties. However, the tables have been turned and it can potentially bring decisively unequal results. A favor is to be met with another favor as opposed to neglect.

The inequality comes when a small initial favor produces an obligation to return a substantially larger favor. From the previous discussions, you have seen how the reciprocity rule can give you space to choose the nature of the first favor and also the nature of the debt cancelling return favor. When pitted against those who have an intention to exploit the rule, we can easily be manipulated into an unfair exchange.

The reason why a small favor can cause a larger return favor is the awkward feeling that comes with the state of indebtedness. Many of us find it totally unacceptable and disagreeable to be indebted to someone because it weighs heavily on us. From childhood, we are trained to chafe emotionally under the burden of obligation. Because of this reason, we find ourselves returning even larger favors than what we received just to relieve ourselves of the psychological burden inherent in debt.

A person who violates this rule is also likely to be segregated by the social group. This distaste that comes from an individual who fails to conform to the reciprocity rule makes it so undesirable that people at times agree to unequal exchanges just to dodge such feelings and possibilities of external shame.

In order to succeed in the reciprocity rule, you need to be tactical. The rejection-then-retreat technique allows you to use an initial concession as part of a larger and highly effective compliance approach. Also known as the door-in-the-face technique, this approach is executed by making a larger request which will most likely be turned down. Thereafter, make a smaller request which was from the beginning your target request. The second request will be seen more of concession and as such you will feel obliged to comply.

3: Leveraging on Commitment and Consistency

In the words of Leonardo Da Vinci, *it is easier to resist at the beginning than at the end*. In a study that was done by Knox and Inkster, Canadian psychologists, discovered something fascinating about the behavior of people at the racetrack. Just before bets were placed, the confidence level the people had on their respective horses and their chances of winning was relatively low.

However, immediately after placing the bets, their confidence levels rose significantly. Despite the fact that the horses were the same and the track did not change, in the minds of the bettors the moment they purchased the ticket, their prospects improved significantly.

This dramatic shift of mind is linked to a common weapon of social influence. Just like the other weapons, it lies deep inside us and directs our actions quietly. This weapon is the desire to be consistent with what we have already done. If you make a choice or take a particular stand, you will encounter both interpersonal and personal pressures to behave in a manner consistent with that commitment.

Those pressures will make you respond in ways that truly justifies your earlier decision. It is simply a way of convincing yourself that you have made the right choice and you have no slightest doubt about your decision. However, these beliefs and commitments may not be realistic at all times. For instance, immediately after they cast their vote, most electorates believe strongly that their candidate will carry the day.

Psychologists have studied and understood the power of consistency and its role in directing people's actions. Famous theorists including Theodore Newcomb, Leon Festinger and Fritz Heider viewed the desire to be consistent as a strategic motivator of behavior. The tendency to be consistent is strong enough to compel us to do things that we would ordinarily not do.

The desire to be consistent constitutes a potent weapon of social influence and oftentimes causes us to act in certain ways that are clearly contrary to our best interests.

In a study that was done in New York City, the researchers staged thefts to see how onlookers will respond. In one part of the study, the researchers who pretended to be thieves strolled down and grabbed some things at random and later walk away. The onlookers did not do anything much, as a matter of fact only a few of them risked their personal lives to chase after the purported thieves.

The other part was conducted in an environment where someone would ask another to watch over his things and then the researcher "thief" would stroll and pick the things being watched over. The result was significantly different because this time the thieves were pursued by the people entitled with the responsibility to guard the things. This simply means that if a person has taken a responsibility and made a choice, they will under all circumstances fight to keep that commitment and consistency.

Consistency is a valued attribute and the person whose words, beliefs and deeds do not match is commonly seen as confused, mentally ill and two-faced. A high degree of consistency is associated with intellectual and personal strength.

The heart of logic, stability, rationality and honesty lies in a consistent personality. Michael Faraday, the Great British Chemist once said that the extent to which being consistent is approved is sometimes much more than being right. Most of the time, you will be better off if your approach to things is characterized by consistency. Without consistency, our lives would be erratic, difficult and disjointed.

Automatic Consistency

Since it is in your best interest to be consistent, there is a likelihood of falling into the habit of automatic consistency even in situations where such consistency turns disastrous.

Just like other forms of automatic responding, automatic consistency offers a desirable shortcut through the complexities of contemporary life. The moment you make up your mind about a particular issue, stubborn consistency becomes very appealing so as to stick to your course.

You will find it unnecessary to think hard about the same issue, sift through a blizzard of information in an attempt to establish the relevant facts as well as expend your mental energy to weigh the merits and demerits. Instead when confronted with the issues, you will immediately play your consistency tape and know what to say, do or believe. You only believe or do what is consistent with your earlier decision.

Consistency allows you a relatively effortless, convenient and efficient method for handling complexities of daily life. This is why it is so difficult to curb consistency as a reaction. It gives you a way of evading the rigors of continuing thought.

As long as your consistency tape is running, you can engage in your daily activities happily knowing that you do not have to think too much. According to Sir Joshua Reynolds – There is no expedient to which a man will not result to avoid the real labor of thinking.

A Shield against Thought

Automatic consistency shields us against engaging thought processes. Because of this, profiteers have devised ways of exploiting such consistency so as to make us respond to their requests without thinking. They arrange to have us play our consistency tapes so as to profit them without us knowing that we are being taken advantage of. Just like in Jujitsu, they fashion and structure their interactions so that our need to be consistent can directly lead to their benefit.

Exploiting Consistency to Enhance Off-Peak Sales

In order to reduce problems caused by seasonal buying patterns, large toy manufacturers employ this approach to psychological intelligence and the power of influence. The main problem of the toy manufacturers is that their sales go into a slump during low seasons. Most of their customers have no money during this period to buy their toys and their budgets are stiffly resistant. In order to solve the problem, the manufactures need to pursue approaches that retain a healthy demand for toys during the off-peak months.

To motivate post-holiday spent out parents to buy extra toys for their children, toy manufacturers can embrace and exploit the powerful force of consistency resident in the parents. Most manufacturers advertise toys prior to the peak season. But because their intention is to sell these toys in the off-peak season, they undersupply the stores during the peak months. When children see the toys on TV ads, they desire them and ask their parents to buy it for them. The parents in turn make a promise to buy them only to go to the stores and find that the toys are not available. To make up for this, they buy substitute toys.

Immediately after the peak season, the manufactures run the ads again and this arouses the desire in the children once more. To live up to their promise, the parents visit the stores and buy the toys. This way, the manufacturers seize the opportunities to sell both in the peak and off-peak season.

The Importance of Commitment

The power of consistency is very important in directing the course of human action. However, to engage this force, you need commitment. In order to make a commitment, you will have to set the stage for your automatic consistency and take a stand. This will evoke a natural tendency to behave in such a manner as to be stubbornly consistent with the stand you have taken.

Commitment strategies are important to anyone who wants to make others comply with his request. The procedures which are designed to create commitment take different forms. There are those that are straightforward while others are very subtle.

To illustrate a straightforward commitment approach, consider Jackson Stanley who is a used cars sales manager. While running a campaign called Used Car Merchandising, he advised his team of 100 sales dealers as follows – Put them on paper.

Have the customers sign on the paper. Get the money first. Control them and ask if they would buy the vehicle if the price is made right. Ensure you pin them down. Being an expert in car merchandising, Stanley believes that when a customer commits to purchase and even pays an upfront, it becomes easier to make them comply.

In addition to the example above, there are some commitment practices that need more finesse in order to be effective. For instance, if you wanted to increase the number of people for a door to door fundraising for charity in your area, you can start by taking a survey asking how many of them would be willing to spend a few hours collecting money for a charitable institution.

Since many of them consider charity a worthy cause, they would not mind responding to the affirmative. Using this commitment, you can then recruit them to help you with your fundraising activity.

What Makes Commitment Effective

The ability of commitment to shape your future behavior is dependent upon a number of factors. To illustrate the factors at play, consider the following example.

At the time of the Korean War, lots of American soldiers who had been captured found themselves as prisoners of war in camps which were managed by Chinese communists. The Chinese treated captives in a different manner than they did to their allies, the North Koreans. Instead of the harsh punishment, the Chinese used a lenient policy which was actually a sophisticated and concerted psychological assault on the captured soldiers. After the war ended, American psychologists who were interested in the Chinese prisoner of war program, questioned the returning prisoners in order to determine what really occurred in the camps.

For instance, hardly any American soldier escaped because any attempt to do so was thwarted by the Chinese who offered a bag of rice to anyone who would turn the prisoner in. This made it easier for all the captured American soldiers to corporate with the authorities.

A closer examination of the program that was used in the camps revealed a heavy reliance on commitment and consistency in order to gain the compliance needed from the captives. Since the prisoners had been trained to give their name, rank and serial number, it proved a little bit difficult for the Chinese to extract additional information.

However, they started small and built it up. Gradually and mildly, the American soldiers were asked to make pro-Communists or anti-American statements. Once these minor requests were honored, the authorities took them to higher level requests that were building on the past requests.

Ultimately, the Chinese authorities would make the American captives to collaborate with them by doing things which to them seem trivial but the Chinese authorities were able to turn them to their own advantage. This technique was mainly used to elicit confessions, information and self-criticism during interrogations.

Other groups also used a similar strategy to progressively escalate commitments so as to induce individuals to perform larger favors. According to research, trivial first commitments are sufficient to jumpstart a momentum of compliance. Sales people can use this psychological weapon of influence to obtain large sales by starting with small ones.

The purpose of a small transaction is commitment not profit. This compliance tactic also referred to as the foot in the door technique has been applauded by social scientists including Scott Frazer and Jonathan Freedman.

There is a general agreement among foot in the door experts that you can use small commitments to turn citizens into public servants, prisoners into collaborators and prospective into customers. The only thing you need to do is to get their self image and drag it where you want. If you want them to behave in a manner consistent with a customer, you can drag their self-image into that of a customer. This will change their self view and comply naturally with a wide range of requests which are consistent with this new self image.

The Magic Act to Commitment

The best evidence of someone's true feelings and beliefs comes from their deeds as opposed to their words. By observing closely the actions of others, you can discover who they really are and what they stand for. Researchers have also found out that people themselves use their own behavior to shape their personality and decide what they are like. Once you understand the belief system, you can alter it gradually and make your subjects act according to this altered self-perception.

Once a commitment has been made, the self-image is constantly squeezed from both sides by consistency pressures. On one side, there is pressure to align the self-image to action while on the other side; there is a sneakier pressure to adjust your image according to how others perceive you. Since others see us as people who stand with what we have said or written, another pull or force is initiated so as to bring the self-image in line with our written statement, thereby occasioning commitment and consistency.

4: The Principle of Social Proof

Have you ever wondered why canned laughter is so popular on televisions? It is because they have won their positions through giving the public what they want. According to research, canned merriment causes the audience to laugh longer and more often whenever the humorous material is presented. Additional evidence also indicates that canned laughter is extremely effective for poor jokes.

This is why television executives go to all lengths to introduce laugh tracks in their programs so as to enhance the humorous and appreciative responses of the audience.

The other question that arises is – why does canned laughter work on us the way it does? It is strange that we tend to laugh more at comedy material that is based purely on mechanical fabricated merriment. Even though we know that the jokes are not real, we often find ourselves falling victims.

The principle of social proof can help us understand why canned laughter works on us the way it does. This principle states that – we determine what is correct by finding out what other people think is correct. This principle is especially applicable in determining our decisions on what constitutes correct behavior. We oftentimes consider a behavior to be correct if a majority of people are doing it.

The tendency to see an activity as appropriate especially when others are doing it is very high. There is an unwritten rule that if you want to make fewer mistakes, act according to the crowd. Just like other weapons of influence, social proof may provide a convenient shortcut for determining appropriate behavior but at the same time it can expose you to the schemes and attacks of profiteers.

Canned laughter becomes effective due to the social proof aspect. We often find ourselves responding in a reflexive and mindless fashion because everyone else around us is doing the same. We use the laughter of others to determine what is humorous even if the subject is not as humorous at all. The television executives have realized this and are exploiting it for their own benefit.

Social Evidence

Apart from television executives, there are other people who use social evidence for profit. Bartenders for instance use a few dollar bills to sort their tip jars at the start of an evening so as to simulate tips that other customers have left for them and give the impression to the guests that tipping with folded money is an acceptable barroom behavior.

Advertisers always inform us of how a product is the fastest growing or the largest selling as a way of convincing us that it is good. They use the power of social evidence and proof to convince us that everyone else around us likes the product and so we should join the bandwagon.

Albert Bandura, a psychologist has been instrumental in developing procedures that are based on the principle of social proof. Together with his colleagues, Bandura has shown how people can get rid of phobias and extreme fears through a simple method. In an earlier study, Bandura, Grusec and Menlove sampled nursery school children who were terrified of dogs and made them watch a little boy who was playing with a dog for about 20 minutes every day.

After only 4 days, 67 percent of the children were so much willing to climb into the playpen with a dog and remain there scratching and petting the dog while everyone else was out of the room. After a month, the improvement was even more significant and the children could freely interact with the dogs.

In another study, Bandura and Menlove added a slight twist where instead of using one child playing with a dog, they used more children. What they discovered was astounding. The more the number of children used in the experiment, the higher the consolidation of social proof. This led to a more effective elimination of phobias. These studies also brought to the fore the powerful psychological influence that filmed examples have in changing children's behaviors.

If you want to do an individual experiment of how powerful social proof is, you can simply stand on a busy sidewalk and pick a spot in the sky or a tall building. Stare at the spot for about a minute. You will discover that fewer people if any will join you and probably ask you what you are looking at.

Try the same experiment with a group of friends and you will discover that a crowd of passersby will stop and crane their necks upwards even though they may not be seeing anything up there. This shows the influential power of social proof.

All the weapons of influence have their optimal conditions in which they work. In order to use them effectively or defend yourself against them, it is important that you know their optimal operating conditions. In general, whenever we are unsure of ourselves, whenever the situation is ambiguous and unclear, uncertainty reigns and there is a high likelihood that we shall accept the actions of others as appropriate.

In the event of an emergency, a bystander will be unlikely to help if other bystanders are present. The first and straightforward reason for this is that with several potential helpers present, the personal responsibility of each individual reduces. The second reason which is more psychologically intriguing is based on social proof and involves what is known as pluralistic ignorance effect.

There is a tendency in times of uncertainty to look around and see what others are doing before you can take action. The most unfortunate thing with this is that everybody else around could also be waiting and looking for social evidence. Since no one looks unruffled and unmoved, the overall result would be a crowd of bystanders looking at emergency without any of them acting.

According to Darley and Latane, the state of pluralistic ignorance can reduce an emergency into a mere speculative event. The only person who can help in such a situation is the one who comes from outside and as such uninfluenced by the calm of the crowd.

Scientific Approach to Social Proof

The idea of safety in numbers may not be helpful and as a matter of fact, may diminish the chances of survival for a victim who could have been saved if only one bystander was present. In their experiment, Latane and Darley used their colleagues and students to stage emergency events. They then recorded the response rate of the emergency victims.

In the first case, a college student pretended to be having epileptic seizure. The student received help 85 percent of the time where a single bystander was present. However, in the midst of 5 bystanders, he only received help 31 percent of the time. Someone can easily argue that we live in a cold society while in real sense it is the presence of other bystanders that reduced the response rate to shameful levels.

This has led social scientists to believe that when witnesses are convinced that an emergency exists, there is a greater chance of help being offered. However, in an instance where the bystanders are not totally convinced that a situation is an emergency, the chances of them responding are very minimal. Pluralistic ignorance effect is very strong among strangers because everyone wants to look sophisticated and graceful. A possible emergency can be regarded as a non-emergency and as such putting the victim's life on the line.

How to Devictimize Yourself

Based on our new found understanding, the failure to act by onlookers can be mitigated and increase the chances of receiving aid in the event of an emergency. The reasons why people do not help is because there is no sufficient social proof to classify the problem as an emergency and as such are unsure rather than unkind. People become exceedingly responsive if they are certain of their responsibilities for intervening in a situation.

The moment you understand that the enemy is not the unkindness of the people but rather the level of uncertainty, you can fight off this uncertainty so as to boost the responsiveness. Any time you find yourself in a situation or predicament and are in need of help against all odds, outcries, groaning and moaning may not attract the attention of passersby.

Instead, you can use a signboard with the word help to indicate a state of emergency. In this situation, you should not fear about embarrassment because your life could be at stake and help is what you need the most. Do everything to capture the attention and concern of the passersby.

Isolating one or two people from a crowd and speaking to them directly can also increase the possibility of them responding to your problem much faster as opposed to speaking to an entire crowd. The person will feel the weight of the responsibility and any uncertainties that may exist will be dispelled leading to a quick and effective response.

Wherever you need the attention of an audience therefore, reducing the uncertainty around your subject can produce tremendous results. If it is a product that you are selling and you want as many people as possible to buy it, approaching one person at a time may be more effective than speaking to a crowd at a go.

The principle of social proof is a reality in every area of our lives where persuasion and conviction is required. Every person is waiting for the other to go first and this may result into the pluralistic ignorance effect which hinders compliance.

Using Similarity to Gain Social Proof and Compliance

In addition to eliminating uncertainty, social proof can be enhanced through similarity. According to a research done in 1954 by Festinger, observing the behavior of ordinary people just like us can give us an insight in what constitutes correct behavior. We are more inclined to follow the trend established by a similar individual than one who is dissimilar.

This is why most TV commercials tend to use an average and ordinary person so that we can easily identify with them even as they use and advocate for a product. The ordinary viewers who compose the largest market share for almost every product are easily convinced if the person at the center of advertisement shares a similar content with them.

A group of psychologists (Hornstein, Fisch and Holmes) from the University of Columbia carried out a study on the compelling evidence brought about by similarity. In the research, the psychologists placed wallets in various locations on the ground. Each wallet had a $2 in cash and a check worth $26.

Inside each wallet was also a note that provided information on the name and address of the owner of the wallet. There was a letter in every wallet addressed to the owner by a person who had earlier found the wallet and had an intention of returning it. The wallets were wrapped in envelops. This indicated that the wallet had been lost the second time on its way to the owner.

The researchers wanted to know how many people would actually follow the example of the first finder and mail the wallets to their owners. One element that was varied in these wallets was the kind of English that was used in the letter. In some, the English was American while in others it was broken and seemed like it was written by a foreigner.

The aim of this variable was to see how many Americans would respond because of the similarity of the finder with their own American culture. According to the results of the study, only 33 percent of the wallets with a dissimilar (foreign) first finder were returned. On the contrary, 70 percent of the wallets where the letters were written in American English (similar) were returned.

This shows one thing that we use the actions of others to determine on the proper rules of behavior especially when we view the other people as being similar to ourselves. Teenagers are often said to be independent-minded and rebellious.

However, it is important to recognize that most of them take after their parents or guardians because they conform to the similarity dimension of social proof. Their parents are their standard of behavior and by default they copy them.

5: Influencing People through the Power of Friendship

There is a tendency to say yes or consent to requests made by people that you either know, like or both. This simple rule has been used for hundreds of years by strangers so as to get compliance with their requests. One of the clear demonstrations of the liking rule or the power of friendship is in the Tupperware parties.

The mechanics at play in these events revolve around peer selling. Trades are arranged around friends which makes it irresistible because the power of friendship supersedes any buy transaction. The party hostess usually calls her friends for a demonstration in her home and capitalizes on the power of psychological selling to influence almost everyone who comes for the party.

Tupperware Home Parties Corporation makes arrangements for its customers either to buy from a friend or for a friend instead of an unknown sales person. In this manner, the warmth, the attraction, the security and the obligation that comes with friendship are brought to bear on the sales approach.

The strength of the social ties between the hostess and the party goers is twice as likely to determine the purchase of the product when compared to the preference for the product itself.

The most interesting thing is that the customers are fully aware of the strategy used by Tupperware but still continue to buy because the power of friendship is stronger. This sales approach has made Tupperware Corporation to abandon retail sales outlets and instead push for home party concept.

According to professionals who have studied the aspect of compliance, they have found that the friend does not necessarily have to be present for the approach to be effective; mentioning his name is enough. One of the effective ways of using the power of friendship to push your products or convince customers is through the endless chain method. In this approach, the customer who has admitted to liking the product is pressed into giving names of friends who would also appreciate learning about the product. The salesperson then reaches out to those friends and from them he gets another list of friends hence the endless chain of names.

The key to success in the endless chain method is that a potential customer is visited by a salesperson who introduces himself as having been referred by a friend of the prospect. This approach makes it difficult for him to be turned away because in doing so, it becomes more or less like rejecting a friend. Research shows that this kind of selling gets a very high compliance rate and comprises 50 percent of the sales effort even before the salesperson speaks.

Factors that Influence Liking:

Physical Appearance

It is generally acknowledged that handsome and beautiful people have an advantage when it comes to social interactions. Recent findings indicate that the response to attractive people is more or less automatic without forethought.

The response falls into a class which social scientists call halo effects. Simply defined, a halo effect occurs when a positive attribute or characteristic of a person dominates the way in which that person is viewed by other people. Physical attractiveness is a characteristic that can overshadow everything else about a person.

Good looking individuals are automatically assigned favorable traits such as kindness, intelligence, honesty and talent even if in real sense they do not have it. A study that was done in 1974 on the Canadian federal elections found that good looking and attractive candidates received over two and half times as many votes compared to their unattractive peers. The strangest thing is that the voters in question did not realize that they were biased. As a matter of fact, 73 percent of the voters surveyed denied that their voting pattern had been influenced by physical appearance.

An effect similar to that of voting has been found in hiring situations. In one study, it was shown that good grooming of the applicants enhanced their chances of being hired compared to their qualifications. This advantage extends beyond the hiring line into payday. Economists examining Canadian and United States job compensation found that good looking individuals commanded a higher salary of up to 12 percent more than their co-workers.

The judicial process is also susceptible to general body appearance. Good looking people are considered to be friendly and hence they get a favorable treatment even in the legal system. In a study done by Stewart in 1980, the researchers noted that handsome men received sentences that were significantly lighter than the rest. The likelihood of unattractive defendants to receive jail sentences was higher than that of their good looking counterparts.

A study done by Chaiken in 1979 demonstrated that attractive people tend to get help faster whenever they are in need. They are also more persuasive in changing the opinions of other people. It can be affirmed that physical attractiveness enjoys enormous social advantage in our present culture.

This halo effect of physical attractiveness is exploited greatly by compliance professionals. Sales training programs have been remodeled to include grooming hints; fashion shops carefully select their floor staffs among the good looking candidates to enhance foot traffic.

Similarity

Since most people have average looks, the physical attractiveness factor may not be much of an influence in triggering compliance. Similarity is another factor that produces liking. We generally like people who are similar to us. This is according to a research done by Bryne in 1971. The similarity can either be in opinion, background, personal traits or lifestyle.

Dressing is one of the examples in similarity. There is a tendency to like people who are dressed like us. In a study done in the 1970s, young people dressed in straight or hippie attire went around campus asking other students for a dollar or two to make a phone call. Whenever the students approached a similarly dressed counterpart, their request was granted faster than in other cases.

Requesters or people seeking compliance from us can easily manipulate us by claiming to have similar backgrounds and interests to ours. For instance, car salespersons are trained to gather evidence from every little thing around about the customer to create similarity.

When they spot camping gear, they may suggest how they would love to go camping in the countryside. When they see golf balls, they may tell you how it feels to tee off on a cool summer day just to bring your interest and theirs on the same page.

In 1979, Brewer found out through a study that customers were more likely to buy insurance whenever the salesperson that made the presentation is like them as far as politics, religion and age are concerned. Even small similarities can be effective in evoking a desired response. Many sales training programs are centered on the mirror and match concept. They do this to present a salesperson who is much like you in every dimension.

Compliments

We can easily comply when we get information that someone fancies us. Oftentimes when people flatter us, we tend to yield to their demands almost unconsciously. In a study done in North Carolina among a group of men, it was found that people generally become helpless in the face of praise. The men received comments about how they looked from people who needed a favor from them. A large number of them complied even without thinking twice.

Cooperation and Contact

Familiarity plays a key role in decision making whether political, social or commercial. Many voters tend to elect a person whose name is familiar. For instance, in one controversial election in Ohio, a candidate who had a lower chance of winning the attorney general race emerged victorious when he changed his name to Brown shortly before the Election Day. Brown just happens to be a name that is very familiar in Ohio and many people can easily identify with this name.

In most cases, we do not realize that our own attitudes are affected by something if we are exposed to it a number of times in the past. If several faces are flashed on a screen and one tends to be flashed several times compared to the others, a greater liking develops for such a familiar face not because of physical attractiveness but the frequency with which it is seen. Since liking has an impact on social influence, the person whose face appears so many times on the screen will most likely persuade the opinions of many individuals.

People are naturally disposed towards the things they have had contact with. Through the contact approach, where individuals from different ethnic backgrounds are presented as equals with more exposure to one another, those individuals will ultimately come to like each other.

Before assuming that cooperation is such a powerful cause of liking, it helps to first pass it through an acid test. You have to determine whether compliance practitioners use cooperation systematically to make us like them so that we can consent to their request or manufacture it when it is not present.

Compliance professionals are continuously attempting to establish a common platform between us and them so that they can convince us we are working for the same goals and as such we must pull together for mutual benefit. By making their subjects as teammates, these practitioners can easily win their support and approval.

Conditioning and Association

There is a natural tendency in human beings to hate or dislike a person who brings unpleasant information even if the person concerned does not have anything to do with the bad news. A study done by Manis, Cornell and Moore indicates that a simple association with bad news is enough to stimulate dislike.

The principle of association governs both positive and negative connections. An extension of this principle guides our social relationships. For instance, even if you did nothing bad, a mere association with bad company is enough to earn you the label of a bad person. People generally assume that we take the same personality as our friends.

In the sales and marketing arena, positive associations are being used by marketing professionals to make us buy their products. They use good looking models so as to influence our decision about the quality of the product being marketed. In essence, the advertiser is hoping that using the models will lend their positive traits of desirability and beauty to their products.

In 1985, Bierley, McSweeniy and Vannieuwkerk carried out a study which showed how the association principle can stimulate us unconsciously to part with our money. In the modern life, credit cards have become an important component in our transactions. The credit card issuers allow us to immediately get the benefits of goods and services while deferring the costs to those goods weeks into the future. This has made consumers to associate credit cards with the positive rather than the undesirable aspects of spending.

Due to the success of the association principle many manufacturers have linked their products with the cultural age. During the late1960s when the American space program was the talk of the nation, everything was branded with its theme from breakfast drinks to deodorants.

In the political circles, candidates have discovered the power of celebrities to sway voters. As such, they are increasingly using them to gain political mileage.

Companies spend millions of dollars to win sponsorships for major sporting events such as the Olympics. They also spend much more in advertisements so as to create a connection with the event. According to a survey conducted by the Advertising Age Magazine, about one third of the consumers interviewed said they would purchase an item as long as it was linked to the Olympics.

The luncheon technique which is an offshoot of the association principle uses the concept of elegant dinners and sumptuous breakfasts to sway the support of people. Most political fundraising campaigns involve food at some point because any association with food brings memories of satisfaction and happiness.

In an experiment done by Razran in 1940, the subjects were presented with a number of political statements which they had earlier rated. At the end of the experiment, Razran established that only the statements that had been shown while food was being served or eaten had gained approval. The change in liking was unconscious and it was linked to the food that was being served. The luncheon technique works in either way. If people are from an unpleasant experience, showing them political statements or slogans is likely to attract disapproval.

The power of friendship and liking therefore is an effective strategy that can be used to gain compliance. Friendship creates social interactions that unite us mentally with the requestor and this makes compliance easy.

6: Authority and Obedience

Whenever we encounter a potent motivator of human action, it is almost natural to expect that there are good reasons for the existence of the motivation. From birth, we are trained to believe that obedience to authority is the right thing and disobedience is wrong.

This message usually fills the school rhymes, parental lessons, songs of our childhood and is even carried forward in military, legal and political systems that we come across as adults. There is much value accorded to notions of submissions and loyalty to legitimate rule.

Religious organizations contribute to the concept of authority and obedience through their teachings. In the first book of the Bible, it is described how the failure to obey God's ultimate authority resulted in such a huge loss for Adam, Eve and the entire human race. In total obedience to God, Abraham was willing to plunge a dagger through Isaac's heart without giving it a second thought. In this story and many others, it can be seen clearly that the correctness of human action was not judged by harmfulness, senselessness or injustice considerations but rather through a mere command of a higher authority.

Stories of obedience teach us the power and the value that authority is given in our society. It is not always that obedience to authority is the right thing because if the authority is wrong then everything else takes after it. Obedience is often an automatic response rather than a conscious deliberation. Information that comes from a recognized authority provides a valuable shortcut for decision making and how to act in a particular situation.

Conforming to authoritative figures such as parents and teachers had its own advantages to us as young children. This is because these people knew much more than we did and taking their advice was very beneficial. The greater wisdom that was in their statements and the weapons of punishment and rewards combined to make us totally obedient.

As adults, we continue to enjoy the same benefits through the authority of figures such as judges, employers and government leaders. Their positions characterize great access to power and information making it logical to comply with their wishes so as to get the rewards and escape the punishment.

When considering the weapons of influence, the same pattern of behavior is applicable. The moment we realize that obedience to authority is rewarding, it becomes simpler for us to allow ourselves to automatically obey. This can at times result into blind obedience which has its own blessings and curses. Since we do not have to think when exercising obedience, we act sheepishly. This can be classified more as a reaction rather than thinking.

The Example of Medicine and Health

The pressures of authority are more visible and strong in the area of medicine and health. It is undeniable that anything touching in health is of enormous importance to us.

Physicians who possess extensive knowledge in the area of medicine automatically become influential and hold the position of respected authorities in our lives.

Health workers understand their positions and level of their jobs. They know that the managing director seats at the top and no one can overrule the decision and judgment of a doctor except one who is at a higher rank than him. This in turn establishes a tradition of automatic obedience to doctor orders among healthcare staffs.

The problem with this kind of hierarchy is when the physician makes a mistake and no one below thinks that there is a mistake. Once the legitimate authority has given an order, the subordinates automatically stop thinking and start reacting.

A study done by the US Healthcare Financing Administration revealed that an average hospital had a 12 percent daily error rate in patient medication alone. In as much as there are many other reasons why such errors occur, professors of pharmacy (Neil Davis and Michael Cohen) from Temple University wrote in their book Medication Errors: Causes and Prevention that many of these problems are caused by mindless deference given to the boss.

The point here is that in many situations where a legitimate authority has spoken, even something that would otherwise make sense becomes automatically irrelevant. Instead of considering the entire situation, there is a tendency to respond to only one aspect.

Whenever our behaviors are governed through such an unthinking manner, chances of compliance professionals trying to take advantage of us are very high. In the field of medicine, advertisers have frequently employed the respect given to doctors in our culture by hiring actors to play the role of doctors to speak on behalf of the product.

Content not Connotation

Whenever an authority speaks, we immediately agree but not necessarily to the content rather connotation. Symbols of authority and power trigger compliance even in the absence of genuine substance of authority. Compliance professionals and con artists have taken advantage of this obedience for their own benefit.

For instance, con artists assign themselves titles, wear expensive clothes and bask in the trappings of authority. By simply emerging from an automobile while elegantly dressed is enough to give them whatever title they are after. They understand pretty well that when they are finely dressed, their chances for compliance are extremely high. Each of three symbols of authority that is titles, trappings and clothes has their own significance.

Titles

Titles are considered the most difficult and yet the easiest symbols of authority to acquire. So as to earn a title, you typically need to devote years of work and achievement.

However, it is also possible for somebody who has circumvented the process to acquire a title label and receive the same kind of automatic deference. Actors in TV commercials and con artists have perfected this art. Certain compliance practitioners lie about their titles so as to get their right of way and influence behavior.

The professional intelligences of junior staffs can easily be unhooked in the face of an authoritative directive. Because of an order coming from a person of a higher title, there is automatic obedience to authority. As longer as your title bespeaks authority, no resistance to your ideas will ever be manifested.

Clothes

This is the second kind of authority symbol which can trigger mechanical compliance. Con artists can easily adopt hospital whites, army green, priestly black or police blue depending on the situation they want to take advantage of. When their victims realize that the authority was imposed rather than earned, it is too late and the con artists have fled.

In a study done by Leonard Bickman in 1974, it was revealed that requests which came from figures dressed in authority attire were the most difficult to resist. Regardless of the type of request, so many people obey the requester because of his costume.

A well tailored business suit can evoke a form of deference even from total strangers.

A research study done in Texas arranged for a 31 year old man to break the law by crossing the road against the direction of traffic rights. In some occasions, he was dressed in freshly pressed business suits and a tie to complement. In other instances, he simply dressed in a work shirt and trousers. As the researchers watched, they noticed that every time the man crosses the road when dressed in a suit, a group of children followed him even though he was breaking the traffic law. This showed how authoritative a person can be by simply dressing the part.

The appearance and presentation of a well dressed person are so impressive that the victim overlooks aspects as important as checking the validity of the person before complying with the request.

Trappings

In a study done in San Francisco Bay area, several owners of prestige cars were shown to receive a special kind of deference compared to the others. According to the experimenters, motorists were willing to wait significantly longer for new luxury cars that were crossing the road than older economy model vehicles.

The aura of prestige vehicles was so intimidating that 50 percent of the motorists waited respectfully without touching their horns until the vehicles moved. Trappings not only force us to obey authority and comply with requests, but also do so unexpectedly. It is more of a kneejerk reaction!

7: The Scarcity Rule of Psychological Influence

In the words of G.K. Chesterton, *the way to love anything is to realize that it might be lost*. There is a notion that less is best and loss is worst. Almost everybody is vulnerable to some extent to the scarcity principle.

A survey conducted on undergraduates in Florida State University rated the quality of food in their campus cafeteria to be unsatisfactory. Nine days following the survey, their minds had changed completely and they were now rating the food as significantly better than before. The event which changed their perspective didn't have anything to do with the foods service but rather its availability.

In between the first and second survey, a fire had destroyed their cafeteria and as such could not eat from there for the next two weeks. This made them appreciate the food that they often underrated at the cafeteria.

The scarcity principle also influences collectors of things from antiques to baseball cards as far as the determination of the worth of an item is concerned. There is an unspoken rule which says that if an item is rare or fast becoming rare then it is more valuable.

The phenomenon of precious mistake in the collectibles market shed more light on the principle of scarcity. For instance, a stamp that is carrying a three-eyed likeness of George Washington is considered incorrect and aesthetically unappealing yet it highly sought after. The irony here is that imperfections which would otherwise make for rubbish, gain popularity and make for prized possession as long as they bring along an abiding scarcity.

People seem to be inspired and motivated by the thought of losing something than by the notion of gaining something of equal value. In a survey, college students experienced much stronger emotions when they were asked to imagine losses versus gains in their grade point averages or romantic relationships. Under conditions of risk and uncertainty, the fear and threat of potential loss plays such a huge role in decision making.

Peter Salovey and Alexander Rothman have studied the scarcity principle in the medical arena where people are frequently urged to undergo tests so as to detect existing illnesses. Since these tests involve the risk that a disease could be found and the uncertainty that once found it could be cured, messages emphasizing potential losses are the most effective.

For instance, pamphlets that advises young women to check for breast cancer by conducting self examinations are seen to be more successful if they are accompanied by a statement of what is to be lost if the examination is not done. Smokers also tend to be attentive where warning signs indicate the likely damage and loss to be suffered if they do not quit smoking.

Limited Numbers

The limited number tactic is one of the most straightforward and powerful application of the scarcity principle. This is where a customer is informed that a certain product is in short supply and as such cannot be guaranteed to last long. This is deliberately done to get customers purchasing bigger orders to move stock.

The disappointment of customers registers unmistakably following an announcement that an item is going out of stock. The imminent loss in its availability makes it more attractive. The beauty of the limited number technique is that customers commit to buying items when there is a limited availability. Lots of customers have personally confessed to buying in this manner.

If a customer asks whether there is an additional model in the store, the salesman may deliberately twist the response to indicate uncertainty. However, when he goes and confirms the availability of the item, he comes back with a sales contract and the customer finds himself at a point where he can't say no to the purchase.

Time Limits

The deadline tactic is related in a way to the limited number technique discussed above. This is where an official time limit is imposed on a customer's opportunity as a way of getting his compliance to the offering. People often find themselves doing things they wouldn't care to do simply because of the fact that time is quickly moving out.

A merchandiser can enhance the tendency of customers paying off by publicizing deadlines beyond which interest implications will come into force. For instance, local council governments may announce deadline for payment of land rates as a way of putting a time limit to influence compliance from land owners. Customers are also told that unless they purchase an item at a certain price, they may have to buy it at a higher price later on.

Psychological Reactance

Compliance practitioners frequently rely on scarcity as a weapon of influence. This is particularly the case in directing human action. The sources of power utilized by the scarcity principle come from two major sources. The first one is our weakness for shortcuts. Almost everyone knows that things that are difficult to acquire are typically better compared to those that are easy to get. This means that value is determined based on the availability of a particular item.

The secondary source of power for the scarcity principle is the loss of freedom brought about by the scarcity of opportunities. Since no one wants to lose the freedom, they go to any extent to acquire the product so as to preserve the status quo.

The desire to fight against restrictions of freedoms can be traced back to the age of two. According to child psychologists, this age commonly known as the terrible twos has lots of contrary behavior manifested by the children. As early as this, the children seem to have already mastered the art of resistance especially to outside pleasure. You tell them one thing; they proceed to do the opposite.

Because of the crucial change that most children undergo at this time, psychological reactance tends to develop. The children recognize themselves as individuals with their own set of rights. They no longer view themselves as social extensions of the main family but rather identifiable and separate individuals.

This concept of independency brings with it the concept of freedom. An independent person is one who has a wide range of choices to make. The children therefore base their behavior on this new found realization and they explore the length and breadth of the options available.

In teenage years, there is another sort of resistance that emerges. This resistance tends to focus more on the rights rather than the responsibilities. The parents attempt to impose authority at this stage in life can be counterproductive. The teenagers will scheme, sneak and fight tooth and nail to resist any attempts at control.

From the above scenarios, it can be seen that whenever something becomes less available, our desire for it increases because of the limited freedom to have it. Our psychological reactance draws us even closer and causes to want the item more.

Contrary to the fact that our desire to own what is limited only applies to commodities; there is research evidence to point to information as a valuable item as well. In the age in which we are living, our ability to acquire, store and manage information, determines our access to power and wealth. Censorship to access of this information can therefore cause a reactance on our part.

Our response to information that is banned such as radical political rhetoric, pornography and media violence is to want to receive the information to a greater extent compared to our desire before the ban.

This finding about censored information does not imply that the people just want to have the information more than ever before but rather they have come to believe in the information more despite the fact that they have not received it.

In a study done in Purdue University by Fromkin, Zellingar, Speller and Kohn, students were shown some advertisers of a novel. Half of the students received an advertisement that had the phrase "A book for adults only" while the other half received advertisement without this phrase.

The researchers later collected feedback from the students concerning their response towards the book. What they discovered was, the students who received the age restriction advertisement wanted to read the book more than the other lot. From this study, it can be concluded that official censorship only serves to increase the desire of the subjects to access what is banned.

Salesmen have taken advantage of this principle to push products into the market. Instead of doing standard appeals, the salesmen go for exclusive information campaign where they convince storeowners to buy particular products because of an impending scarcity in the immediate future.

The feeling of being in competition for something that is scarce has powerful motivating properties. The appearance of a rival in a love circle particularly where one of the partners is an indecisive lover motivates the incumbent to fight hard to ward off the intruder.

When salespeople try to push a product to a certain undecided target market, they use pretty much the same strategy. For instance, a real estate agent selling a house to fence-sitting prospects may announce that another potential buyer has already seen the house and they are interested in it.

This tactic is often known as goosing them off the fence. It works devastatingly well because the thought of losing out to a rival can turn a hesitant buyer into a zealous one.

Scarcity therefore spurs the desire to buy or acquire an item not because of its merits but due to the fact that the said item may be out of stock sooner. The reasoning transits from rational to emotional and this causes compliance.

8: Automaticity and Instant Influence

Oftentimes when we make a decision about something or someone, we do not use all the available and relevant information. Instead, we use a particular highly representative piece of the whole. An isolated piece of information however representative it may be can potentially lead us to make stupid mistakes.

Despite our vulnerability to make mistakes in our decisions, the tendency to use shortcuts is now greater than ever. This is because of the pressures of the modern life. This kind of automatic response has been traced to lower animals which use it for survival and communication. However, the reason why it is so convenient for these animals to use automaticity in their response mechanism is because of their mental capacity. They have small brains that cannot register and process every bit of information in their environments.

Human beings on the contrary have effective brain mechanisms that can handle complex factors, manipulate them and come up with a more informed conclusion. Nobody challenges us in our ability to take into account a multitude of facts and figures. This information processing advantage is what sets us apart from other species and makes us dominant on this planet.

It must be appreciated that human beings too have their own limitations. For the sake of efficiency, it becomes necessary for us to retreat from sophisticated time consuming and fully informed brand of decision making to a primitive automatic and single-feature type of response. For instance, before you say yes or no to a requester, you may find yourself paying attention to a single piece of information in the situation.

The tendency to use lone cues is much more convenient when we do not have time, energy, inclination or cognitive resources to undertake a complete and thorough analysis of a situation. When we are stressed, uncertain, rushed, distracted, fatigued or indifferent, our focus tends to be less on the information available to us. Making decisions under these circumstances makes us to utilize a single piece of information.

Modern Automaticity

The British economist John Stuart Mill was a political thinker and a science philosopher. Though he passed on in 1873, he is still remembered until today for being the last man to know almost everything in the world.

The information that is available today is less than 15 years old because of its monstrous expansion and multiplicative nature. There are fields where knowledge is said to double once every eight years. This rapid growth in knowledge and information is likely to continue since more and more researchers are pumping their newest findings into more than 4,000 scientific journals worldwide.

The rate at which issues considered important on the public agenda are changing is amazing. The shelf life of information is much shorter as observed in a study done by McCombs and Zhu in 1995. Nowadays, we travel faster, relocate more frequently to new places and contact more people than it was in the past. Transience, acceleration, diversity, and novelty are acknowledged as prime descriptors of a civilized existence.

The avalanche of information and options is made possible through the burgeoning technological progress. Our ability to collect, store, retrieve and disseminate information has improved significantly.

The modern day visionaries such as Bill Gates agree that indeed we are living in an era where devices capable of delivering a universe of information to anyone, anytime and anywhere is possible. We are living in the information age where those who need information can access it without much of sacrifice. This information however does not translate directly into knowledge because it must first be processed before being integrated and retained.

Shortcuts and the Challenges of Modern Life

Because technology evolves much faster compared to our own speed of evolution, our natural capacity to process information is fast becoming inadequate to handle the abundance of choice and change. Our creation of a complex world has resulted into a deficiency which makes us take shortcuts to achieve a given goal.

Compliance is based on partial analysis of factors because we cannot consider everything at the same time. This paralysis of analysis has made us to revert to only a single and unreliable feature in our analysis.

Compliance practitioners have used trickery to profit from the mechanical and mindless nature of shortcut responding. Since the frequency of shortcut responding is fast increasing with the form and pace of modern life, it is only objective to state that trickery is also destined to increase at the same rate.

As an example of our frequently used shortcuts, consider the principle of social proof which says that we do what other people like us are doing. In most cases, what is popular within a given situation is also appropriate and functional.

An advertiser who provides information without deceptive statistics about a brand offers us valuable evidence about the quality of the product. If we are in the market for that product, we may want to rely on that bit of information in making our purchases.

This kind of shortcut approach into making decisions conserves our cognitive energies so that they can be used in dealing with the rest of our decision-overloaded and information-laden environment.

The story changes when an advertiser capitalizes on this automaticity to give us a raw deal. He may create an image of popularity for a particular product using actors who pose as ordinary citizens and professionals. This evidence of popularity is counterfeit and can easily mislead us into making wrong purchase decisions.

Seeking compliance by leveraging on our reliability on shortcuts is ethically wrong. However, with the blitz of modern daily life, rules of thumb and shortcuts are the order of the day. There is therefore a need to retaliate whenever we come across an individual who betrays our rules of thumb for profit.

Conclusion

In the society, everyone is alive through the battle for influence. Each day that passes, exposes us to innumerable persuasion attempts from interest groups, corporations, political parties or even friends and families. Each one of these compliance practitioners try to persuade us to buy into their ideal, product or innovation.

The supremacy of our viewpoints, actions and ideals is what draws others around us. As a matter of fact, each one of us plays the influence game to a certain degree. Psychologists have been particularly concerned with how human beings influence each other and obtain compliance even in situations where they should not have succeeded.

It is a wonderful experience to take part in an adventure of persuading others and sweeping them up into an unexpected idea, action or unproven vision. The ability to create a sensation and excitement around you is what makes you a great compliance practitioner. As a leader, you cannot do without the power of persuasion.

You may be eloquent and powerful but without a compelling and convincing ability, your leadership may not have a great impact. Persuasion and its mastery is not for the fainthearted but the good thing is that if you care enough to ignite a spark and watch it glow into a flame, the outcome will be inevitable.

Persuasion is a form of communication which must be learned just like any discipline. It helps you to focus on the response you will evoke rather than on the words you will say to counter the reluctance of others. To succeed in persuasion and psychological influence, you must be prepared to express your own keenness, excitement and the leaps you have made all the way from logic to an imaginative new proposition.

Psychological influence is not about swaying people against their will but rather giving them a chance to see things from a new perspective. Therefore, as the initiator, you have to find a delivery style that will make it possible for you to communicate your conviction in an inescapable and compelling way.